CLASS WARRIOR—TAOIST STYLE

Wesleyan Poetry

CLASS WARRIOR

Abdelkébir Khatibi

Translated by Matt Reeck

Wesleyan University Press | Middletown, Connecticut

— TAOIST
STYLE

Wesleyan University Press
Middletown CT 06459
www.wesleyan.edu/wespress
English translation © 2017 by Matthew Stefan Reeck.

First published in France under the title *Le lutteur de classe
à la manière taoïste* by Abdelkébir Khatibi. Copyright
Abdelkébir Khatibi, 1976. Published by permission of the
Estate of Abdelkébir Khatibi.

Library of Congress Cataloging-in-Publication Data

Names: Khatibi, Abdelkebir, 1938– author. | Reeck, Matt, translator.
Title: Class warrior—Taoist style / Abdelkebir Khatibi ; translated
    by Matt Reeck.
Description: Middletown, Conn. : Wesleyan University Press, 2017. |
    Series: Wesleyan poetry | "English translation (c) 2017 by Matthew
    Stefan Reeck"—Verso title page. | Originally published in French
    as Le lutteur de classe à la manière taoïste.
Identifiers: LCCN 2017019106 | ISBN 9780819577528
    (cloth : alk. paper) | ISBN 9780819577535 (pbk. : alk. paper)
Subjects: LCSH: Khatibi, Abdelkebir, 1938—Translations into English.
Classification: LCC PQ3989.2.K4 A2 2017 | DDC 841/.914—dc23
LC record available at https://lccn.loc.gov/2017019106

5   4   3   2   1

CONTENTS

INTRODUCTION

Abdelkébir Khatibi (1938–2009) is considered one of the most prominent writers of postcolonial Francophone literature from North Africa. His list of works includes thirty-six separate titles, and during his lifetime he won literary and intellectual prizes in Morocco and France. Despite the fact that he was a trained sociologist, Khatibi described himself as a poet, saying, "I don't consider myself a thinker or a philosopher or a critic, even if I often use this or that philosophical or scientific concept. For me, I strive in the direction of the 'poem.'"[1]

Khatibi grew up in several cities—first El Jadida, then Marrakech and Casablanca. He wrote about these years in his first major literary work, *La mémoire tatouée* (*Tattooed Memory*), an experimental autobiography.[2] He recalls the experience of having his father die when he was seven years old, and how he was subsequently trundled between his mother's household and that of a loving aunt. It was during these years, he speculates, that he developed an intellectual sensibility that favored multiplicity, the intercultural, and a bearing toward the world and its diversity. In *La mémoire tatouée*, he wonders self-consciously, "The orphan of a father who had disappeared and two mothers, would I have a sort of toggle set inside me?"[3] Later, in *Le scribe et son ombre* (The scribe and his shadow), a work published one year before his death, he declares: "This multipolar tendency . . . nourished in me a strong feeling of uncertainty that, by chance, orphaned me of any spiritual master who would have guided my education."[4] It would be hard to overemphasize the figure of the orphan in understanding Khatibi's life and work as it provides him with the poetics that shaped much if not all of his literary production.

In 1959 Khatibi left Morocco for Paris to attend graduate school; he finished his PhD in sociology at the Sorbonne in 1965. His dissertation was devoted to a sociological reading of the Maghrebi novel in French, the first work to deal with the subject. The three men who sat on his thesis committee were Roland Barthes; René Etiemble, an important figure in the history of the discipline of comparative literature in France; and his principal advisor, Jacques Berque, a prominent sociologist of North Africa.

Khatibi traveled extensively during his time in Europe, then returned to live in Morocco in 1964. There he hoped to lead a new generation of postcolonial sociologists who could tackle the formidable task of describing Moroccan society on its own terms, outside of Orientalist paradigms. In 1966, he became the director of the Moroccan Institute of Sociology, a post he held until the institute dissolved four years later. Also in 1966, he took up editing a central periodical of Moroccan colonial and postcolonial intellectual life, the *Bulletin économique et social du Maroc* (The economic and social bulletin of Morocco), a responsibility that he held until 2004.[5]

He began his teaching career at Mohammed V University in Rabat in 1969, where he continued to work until his untimely death in 2009. Barthes taught there as well in 1969–70, when the two men lived across the street from each other. It was during this time that Barthes proposed a semiotic project on Moroccan traditional dress, which Khatibi declined "with regret"[6] because he was in the throes of writing *La mémoire tatouée*.

In September 1974, Khatibi's circle of important friends would expand again. That year he met Jacques Derrida at a café in front of Saint-Sulpice in Paris. They would exchange books—Derrida giving his new acquaintance *Glas*, and Khatibi returning the favor with *La blessure du nom propre* (The wound of identity) and *Vomito blanco*.[7] The two would remain friends until Derrida's death in 2004.[8]

While Khatibi admitted that Paris was his second home,[9] the fact that he did not remain there is significant. Many intellectuals from the decolonizing world who travel to the colonial center do not resettle in their homeland. Khatibi's reasons for returning to Morocco were professional, personal, and perhaps something more enigmatic. "This country has a real life to it," he writes. "I owe it my birth, my name, my initial identity. How could I not love it with benevolence? A critical and vigilant benevolence. A homeland isn't only the place where a person comes into the world, but a personal choice that gives a sense of belonging."[10]

Morocco also provided him with a felicitous distance from the polarizing effects of Parisian intellectual life, with its constant backbiting and changes of allegiance, the hyperbole and caricature of its professional and literary coteries. Recalling the hotly contested debates over structuralism in the 1960s, Khatibi writes:

> I lived in Morocco, out of the fray. While keeping up with the intense activity that was called "structuralism," I didn't feel involved in the back and forth play between the various positions. I observed at a distance these battles that raged on and off between the eminent spirits of Paris, each who wished to think better and faster than the others. My marginality protected me; it was an agreeable shelter.[11]

In this passage, the word "distance" instructs us on how to read his work. We should not assume that Khatibi wished to participate in these debates as a sort of geographically, socially, and intellectually distant commentator. Khatibi never wanted that. Instead, his chosen position resembles that of a tinkerer—a *bricoleur*, in the lingo of Claude Lévi-Strauss and Jacques Derrida—a pragmatic itinerant with his rattlebag of tricks. Khatibi was a writer for whom allegiance to any particular intellectual path was not an overweening concern: "I read all philosophers out of school, out of their traditional context. I'm unaffiliated in this way."[12] The ideas that circulated in the air of French intellectual life were certainly important to him, and he used them. But when we bear in mind the considerations that inform his life in Morocco, we can see his choice to live there as revealing of a fierce sense of independence.

Khatibi's regard for Morocco was not without the critical sensibility that defines his life and work in general; even so, the land of his birth provided him with a commodious home. In 1990 he would marry Lalla Mina El Alaoui. They had two children, Ahmed and Chama.

A POET'S LEGACY AND THE POETICS OF THE ORPHAN

Khatibi's work is held in high regard in Francophone circles and generally received with ignorance elsewhere. For a writer with such a large bibliography, friends of such celebrity, and an oeuvre that speaks to many of the central concerns of postcolonial and postmodern life, the fact that Khatibi isn't better known outside of Francophone scholarship is curious.[13] No doubt, part of that relative obscurity is due to his having lived in Morocco, as the simple fact remains that writers who reside in the sites of political and literary power are more often rewarded with greater visibility—and vice versa. But in the Anglophone context, and even in the French metropolitan context, Khatibi's legacy has suffered from his association with writers who have achieved greater renown.

Edward Said, for example, infamously dismissed Khatibi. Speaking of him in a 1998 interview with Stephen Sheehi in the Los Angeles magazine *Al-Jadid: A Review and Record of Arab Culture and Arts*, Said observes, "Khatibi is a nice guy but peripheral. He is perceived as a kind of Moroccan equivalent of Derrida. But he doesn't have the force or the presence of the place or the location inside French culture that Sartre or Foucault do or had."[14] Said's disregard for Khatibi, a writer with concerns resembling his own, seems almost inexplicable. His remarks smack of condescension.

In hindsight, Said missed a chance to appreciate Khatibi for what he does best. Part of Khatibi's difficulty in finding a more welcoming readership relates to the difficulty of his work, to his style and its tendency to defy categories. He challenges generic conventions and refuses to abide by the protocols of intellectual and academic disciplines. But placing Khatibi in a literary lineage is no less complicated than viewing him as a type of philosopher, as Said does. Khatibi acknowledges that he composed his first poems in Arabic and then in English under the "inescapable influence" of Baudelaire.[15] He also writes of the early importance for him of Victor Segalen, whom he discovered in 1957 and credits with showing him how to "unify anthropology [*ethnologie*] and literature."[16] The citation of Segalen is revealing, not just because Segalen was virtually unknown when Khatibi read him, but also because another seminal postcolonial French-language literary-critical thinker, Edouard Glissant, has acknowledged Segalen's importance as well. Segalen's writings about world cultures—whether in Tahiti or China—stand as an underdeveloped narrative thread in Francophone literature.

I call Khatibi an ontological writer. By that I mean that he played with limits—limits of genre, expression, and identity—as typically inscribed in literary production. Khatibi's admixture of theoretical thinking and creativity, which I call "literary-critical thinking," means that some of his works pose challenges that the run-of-the-mill literary novel, poem, or novella does not. The multiplicity—the tendency toward dispersion, excess, and wandering—that characterizes his oeuvre comes from his personality, reinforced in his psychological makeup by the experiences of his adolescence, then theorized in adulthood. His challenging, polyphonic work should be read within the context of decolonization as well—especially his output from the 1970s, when violence appears as a motif. This violence—the "Very Great Violence," as it appears in *La mémoire tatouée*—is a necessary activity of the decolonizing subject. As Frantz Fanon argued in *Les damnés de la terre*, the refashioning of history, like the refashioning of a national culture, necessitates violence. Khatibi and others in his generation were engaging in an experimental refashioning of their literary inheritance, hoping to escape the conformity of French metropolitan models.[17]

Both in France and in the United States, scholars have relied most heavily upon two texts published in 1983—*Amour bilingue* (*Love in Two Languages*) and *Maghreb pluriel* (The plural Maghreb)—to elucidate Khatibi's views on living between cultures, between languages and, generally, in a state of "in betweenness."[18] His work has been cited in theories of *métissage*, or intercultural identity, and border thinking.[19] The bulk of scholarship on Khatibi is located in excavating, describing, and theorizing his obsession with finding value in the gaps, crossings, and other means of exceeding the parochial dictates of univocal (or polar) conceptions of the self, language, and culture.

In *La mémoire tatouée*, Khatibi writes of growing up in a culture defined by "bricolage" and its imbrication and overlap of cultural values.[20] This work reaches a pinnacle of frustrated self-definition with the phrase, "What a messed-up identity! [Quel bricolage d'identité!]"[21] Elsewhere, Khatibi writes of the position of Moroccan literature as being that of chiasmus—belonging, on the one hand, to the "tradition of the French language" and, on the other hand, to "the mother tongue, the oral tradition, and proverbs."[22]

Khatibi's essays "Pensée-autre" (Other-thinking) and "Double critique" have been regarded as the most direct expressions of his ideas of intercultural living and his most significant attempts at theorizing ways to end the ossified binaries of East and West. The ideas on display there, grouped within the exigencies of his double critique, find their precursor in Khatibi's poetics of the orphan, the operative trope from three important works from the 1970s: *La mémoire tatouée* (1971), *La blessure du nom propre* (1974), and especially *Class Warrior—Taoist Style*. The poetics of the orphan rescues the word "orphan" from the context of the Western metaphysical tradition's obsession with pure presence, or *parousia*, critiqued most famously by Derrida in *De la grammatologie* (*Of Grammatology*).[23] If we renounce the idea of origins, if we reject a belief in the importance of the cultural rooting of our first days, then we will be freed to understand identity as something other than a recursive and conservative mechanism needing constant grounding within an authentic, pure, or original first articulation.[24] In short, Khatibi argues against the idea that there is one "pure" self to which we can resolutely refer and whose stability guarantees us knowledge of ourselves. Self-mastery is never possible, nor is it a goal. Through this lens, the possibilities for a person's growth are as various as the circumstances in which that person lives. The orphan, then, is redeemed as a literary-critical figure who embodies the hopeful and productive possibilities for living in a world governed by diaspora, migration, and intercultural living.

TRANSLATING KHATIBI

Translating Khatibi is not an easy task. His familiarity with a wide range of literary, sociological, and philosophical texts, his lack of disciplinary rigidity, and his freedom from ideological commitment combine to make the currents of his thoughts difficult, at times, to navigate. While Taoism and Marxism stand out conspicuously in the work's title, the influence of the first seems largely limited to a propositional syntax familiar to Taoism[25] and a smattering of ritual terms that embellish the text from time to time. Taoism is not a common point of repair for Khatibi. While a perplexing Chinese fresco appears in the last section of *La mémoire tatouée*, its function there isn't realistic. Rather, it points to something poetic and marvelous—something of fable and myth. Taoism operates in *Class Warrior* in a similar way: as a rhetoric and as a symbolic cache of poetic value.

Marxism likewise presents a nebulous grounding for an authoritative reading of *Class Warrior*. A bevy of lexical items culled directly from the vocabulary of Marxist doctrine and ideology does exist in the text but, as in the case of Taoism, the function of this vocabulary seems more poetic than otherwise. Khatibi was not a staunch Marxist; in 1968, he broke away from the important Moroccan literary-cultural group that published the journal *Souffles* because he felt uncomfortable with its growing Marxist bent. In *Class Warrior*, Marxism's revolutionary connotations are deployed as a means to generate the manifesto-like ethos of the poem.

Khatibi was not a particularly dedicated theorist of translation. His most quoted statements about translation—pitched as a discussion of untranslatability—can be found in his two books from 1983.[26] More pertinent to this text is a comment from *La blessure du nom propre*. In an essay on Moroccan proverbs, he writes that "[to] translate is to veer toward the dissolution of the self in the violent gap between two languages."[27] This definition relates the act of translation to his poetics of the orphan and his theory of identity, both of which he was developing in the 1970s.

Khatibi writes in *Class Warrior* that he teaches "orphan knowledge," "difference without return," and "precision violence." Texts, too, are subject to this framework of knowledge. Like identity, a text is less a uniform whole than a skein of difference that, as Julia Kristeva observes, "takes shape as a mosaic of citations."[28] If each text is a polyglot compendium, talkative and restless, then it makes little sense to fix two texts into the straightjacket of fidelity. The designations of "original" and "translation" deny the intertextuality that Khatibi believes proper to all texts, and the terms serve only to reinvest thinking in the hierarchized dictates of *parousia* that, in this case, delimit the original as the transcendental sign.[29]

In order to abide by the theoretical injunctions that Khatibi lives and writes by, it is necessary to avoid the pointillist comparison of difference between two texts, a comparison that in normative conversations about translation is undergirded by a negative ontology: the one will never "match," "amount to," or "equal" the other, which is pre-inscribed with the values of being the first, pure, complete, and true. Identity does not work this way, Khatibi says, and I argue that his poetics of the orphan correspondingly contains the rejection of a simplistic vision of textuality and translation.

Khatibi didn't think of himself as a systematic thinker—and thus didn't strive for the purported systematicity of philosophers. Perhaps this is why his definition of translation in *La blessure du nom propre* presents one inconsistency: if the self is defined by its internal differences as well as by the violence that is inherent in its continual making and remaking, then how does translation put the self at risk of disappearing? Based on the principles outlined in *Class Warrior* and elsewhere, translation should operate instead with the very flux of movement, turbulence, and the necessary productive violence that defines identity.

It may be that Khatibi found poetic inspiration for his ideas about identity in the intersection of Taoism, Marxism, and semiology.[30] To revolt, to revolve, to evolve: identity can be seen as a force of self-liberation through multiplicity. Extending this notion to the theory of translation frees it from an essentialist paradigm and argues for an intertextuality in which difference is the fundamental constitutive process that, far from standing in the way of meaning, creates it.

Matt Reeck
Brooklyn, New York

NOTES

1. Abdelkébir Khatibi, "Pour une veritable pensée de la différence," interview in *Lamalif* 85 (1977). Quoted in Marc Gontard, *La violence du texte: études sur la littérature marocaine de langue française* (Paris: L'Harmattan, 1981), 81.

2. Khatibi, *La mémoire tatouée* (Paris: Les lettres nouvelles, 1971).

3. Khatibi, *La mémoire tatouée*, 1971 (Rabat: Okad, 2007), 18.

4. Khatibi, *Le scribe et son ombre* (Paris: Editions de la Différence, 2008), 23.

5. The online resources of the Bibliothèque Nationale du Royaume du Maroc show that Khatibi was the chief editor for issues 100 to 163 over the years 1966 to 2004.

6. *Le scribe et son ombre*, 56.

7. Khatibi, *La blessure du nom propre* (Paris: Denöel, 1974) and *Vomito blanco* (Paris: Union générale d'éditions, 1974).

8. Khatibi, *Jacques Derrida, en effet* (Paris: Al Manar, 2007).

9. Ibid., 55.

10. *Le scribe et son ombre*, 9.

11. Ibid., 55.

12. Ibid., 61.

13. To date, only two translations of his works have appeared: *Love in Two Languages*, translated by Richard Howard (Minneapolis: University of Minnesota Press, 1990) and *Tattooed Memory*, translated by Peter Thompson (Paris: L'Harmattan, 2016).

14. Quoted in Françoise Lionnet, "Counterpoint and Double Critique in Edward Said and Abdelkebir Khatibi: A Transcolonial Comparison," in *A Companion to Comparative Literature*, edited by Ali Behdad and Dominic Thomas (London: Blackwell, 2011), 399.

15. *Jacques Derrida*, 55.

16. *Le scribe et son ombre*, 41.

17. See Olivia C. Harrison, "Cross-Colonial Poetics: *Souffles-Anfas* and the Figure of Palestine," *PMLA* 128.2 (2013): 353–69.

18. Two scholars are broadly responsible for the international recognition of Khatibi's literary and theoretic importance: Marc Gontard in France and Françoise Lionnet in America. Their respective work on Khatibi spans three decades. See Gontard, *La violence du texte* and *Le moi étrange: littérature marocaine de langue française* (Paris: L'Harmattan, 1993). His most recent essay "L'Altérité et le métissage: L'entropie ou la créolisation" in *L'autre en mémoire*, edited by Dominique Laporte (Sainte Foy, Quebec: Presses de l'Université Laval, 2006) expands upon that earlier work. See also Lionnet, "'Logiques métisses': Cultural Appropriation and Postcolonial Representation" in *College Literature* 19.20 (1992–93): 100–120, where she cites *Amour bilingue* and *Maghreb pluriel* as influential sources for the conceptualization of transculturation, or how minority writers (writers whose mother tongue is not French) can appropriate French to represent a "hybrid, heteroglot universe" (104). This work is reproduced in her book *Postcolonial Representations: Women, Literature, Identity* (Ithaca: Cornell University Press, 1995). See also Lionnet's "Counterpoint and Double Critique in Edward Said and Abdelkebir Khatibi" in *A Companion to Comparative Literature*, 387–407.

19. See in particular Walter Mignolo, *Local Histories/Global Designs: Coloniality, Subaltern Knowledges, and Border Thinking*, second ed. (Princeton: Princeton University Press, 2012), 66–75.

20. *La mémoire tatouée*, 107.

21. Ibid., 181.

22. Khatibi, "Lettre-Préface," in Gontard, *La violence du texte*, 8.

23. Jacques Derrida, *De la grammatologie* (Paris: Editions de Minuit, 1967).

24. The scholar Mustapha Hamil writes, "Orphan thought allows Maghrebian writers in French to negotiate their way out of the established Arabo-Islamic theological and literary tradition. It also establishes a sufficient detachment from the dogmatism of Eurocentric thought and culture." See Mustapha Hamil,

"Interrogating Identity: Abdelkebir Khatibi and the Postcolonial Prerogative," *Alif* 22 (2002): 84.

25. See Gontard, *La violence du texte*, 81.

26. Emily Apter writes that Khatibi "defines untranslatability as a layered forgetting associated with traumatic memory sequences, erotic fantasies, and intimations of mortality that are unexpectedly triggered by the bilingual unconscious." In her reading, a language of negativity prevails: "Khatibi enacts a seizure of language fear mollified only by amnesia. The 'garlands of phrases, intertwined with death' decorate the tomb of forgetting and exhaustion, which is the bilingual's only hope for peace." She summarizes Khatibi's general stances as "atopic bilingualism." See Apter, "'Untranslatable' Algeria: The Politics of Linguicide," in *The Translation Zone: A New Comparative Literature* (Princeton, NJ: Princeton University Press, 2006), 105–7.

27. *La blessure du nom propre*, 45.

28. James Clifford quoting Julia Kristeva's *Semeiotikè* (Paris: Seuil, 1969). See James Clifford, "Notes on (Field)notes," in *Fieldnotes, the Makings of Anthropology*, edited by Roger Sanjek (Ithaca: Cornell University Press, 1990), 55.

29. Khatibi writes that even the terms "source language" and "target language" "have a limited efficacy [since] they return to the metaphysical designations of the sign, origins, and copy and translation." See *Maghreb pluriel*, 204.

30. Khatibi admits that, by the later 1960s, semiology had replaced sociology in his thinking. See *Le scribe et son ombre*, 47.

CLASS WARRIOR—TAOIST STYLE

1.

history is a word
ideology a word
the unconscious a word
words are like dares
in the mouths of the ignorant

or each sign regenerates
an undeniable freshness
don't get lost in your own thinking
don't disappear into that of others

test the blood of your thinking

because in answer to your question
you will find only quavering targets
action shapes words
like the arc consumes the crystalline arrow

2.

the orphan
is the class warrior
the sovereign orphan

what does "orphan" mean to us?
every hierarchy presupposes
a father a mother and a third
every politics
a master a slave and a third

the historical person is a disgrace

can you disfigure the class enemy
without taking on his likeness?
can you defeat
your own mirages?
everyone cherishes identity
everyone looks for origins
and I teach orphan knowledge

wander the roads
without getting entangled in the weeds

the bird's song
will fail to keep up with your pace
on your lips
the wound will fail to redden the sun

I teach difference without return
and precision violence
that's what "orphan" means

what does "the sovereign orphan" mean to us?
the class warrior never shows off his weapons
he keeps strong and quiet
and destroys with rigor
the person who can do those two things
is my orphan comrade

sovereignty burns
the class warrior
like a straw dog

⸡. inside outside
nearby far away
visible invisible
capital work
this is the class enemy

how to defeat the class enemy?
change your thought categories
and you will change your actions
change your actions
and you will raise up your body
raise up your body
and you will talk with the unthinkable

politics is sensual
a shapeshifting calligraphy
with a rainbow of precise gestures
mark out your destiny

what the iris reflects
erases heaviness
a strict lightness
must command your style

how to defeat the class enemy?
everything that is said
against the class enemy
must be a poison target

4.

when a revolutionary reads Marx
he puts it into effect with vigilance
when a liberal reads Marx
sometimes he keeps it in mind sometimes he forgets
when a fascist reads Marx
he breaks into laughter
if he didn't laugh at all
Marx wouldn't be Marx

but my adage says
the real revolution has no heroes

5.   family undercuts you
love absorbs you
every institution is regressive

practice combinatory lovemaking
this is the secret of every light drunkenness

the before and the after harmonize
the high and the low make anew
the genitals and the butt touch
that's where the body's desires are cut off

I heard it said
that the revolution is universal coitus
but beware of this phrase
beware!

it's better to make love to love
this is the secret of every drunkenness

6.

licit illicit
good bad
presence absence
law transgression
a vacillating symmetry separates them

don't hamper yourself with these cold binaries
the class struggle alters the meaning of number

open yourself to contradictory shades
first blind contradiction
then contradictions dissolve

tactics strategy revolution
three words used when talking
beware
each action invents a dancing hierarchy

the rise and fall of the stars will never end
the human revolution will never stray

how to define your new hierarchy?
by everything that is said

a healer's touch will never calm my particular delirium

ר. I like the gazelle running on the beach

and like a gust of wind I disappear
into the sand and glistening water

and so my metaphor is a vague outline

to each part of your body
give sweet sustenance
at every moment of your life
be active and intractable

living in time is a migratory art

8.   in your gaze there's a strange scratch
I will call this thing color

the occidental appears red and yellow
the oriental appears red and white
if everyone becomes red
what will happen to the rainbow?

the eyelash equal to a sun is too delicate
the jade pin is too nostalgic

so I teach you the orphan voyage

the voyage halted in crystalline drift
volatile desire rips the horizon
bind yourself to difference without return
this is the supreme song of all drunkenness

9.

the eskimo says
you're as desirable as a baby seal
the bedouin says
you're as desirable as a gazelle tattoo
the hindu says
you're as desirable as symmetry
the class warrior says
you're as desirable as a grand revolution

what is a "grand revolution"?
a class never destroys another
like a sandcastle
that's why the revolution is a cannibal
it defeats then absorbs the class enemy

in turning against itself it makes history
in making history it opens up a double universe

while laughing prepare the act of very great violence

10.

the universe is a chessboard
this principle is simple
but no one can know all its ins and outs
it's better to renounce luck

why is this secret so secret?
when you take a pawn you submit to living in time
when you approach living in time madness destroys you

practice while playing the art of the gyre

every stroke of good luck is unjustifiable
this principle is simple
but the vibration here is immense
it's better to cum on top of the class enemy

that's why revolutionary cum
can slide down the throat

every stroke of good luck is unjustifiable
but why?
nothing equals difference without return
nothing stops constant fervor

only the trembling of my lust remains
and when I cry I invite you to share ecstasy

stick to simple hardships
and cherish the other as you break with yourself

to love is to understand better
to understand is to suffer better
to suffer better is to never despair

the class warrior keeps in his breast a piece of jade

11.   why don't you eat with your hands anymore?
why aren't flies pestering you anymore?
now that you're someone the simple ways abandon you

who knows how to stop the drifting of meaning
understands the hierarchy
the one who understands the changing hierarchies
acts according to new values

that's why the class warrior
doesn't jump like a fickle grasshopper

happily he wounds his own class
so practice oblique thinking

12.
truth is a word
found in language

I write these simple words to surprise you
who possesses language controls violence
but the supreme violence exceeds words

make your actions a faltering truth
make your truth a lasting critique

if all the class warriors applied their force
a strange dew would descend upon all peoples

step forward and stop to think
practice the art of the lightning bolt

strike where the luck of the other dazzles you
dig the arrow into the heart of its wound
and strangle the questions that hound you

destiny chips off like a crystal flower

13.

you don't have a soul
you don't have a heart
you don't have a body

soul heart body
empty and sterile categories
if I use the word body
it's because I hate the perversion of the soul
if I use the word heart
it's to test the blood of your thinking

this isn't simple word play
meditate on the gyre of double language

how to make a hierarchy of your body?

on your divided body trace a volatile circle
the most exact rhythm rejects right and left
the most intoxicating symmetry destroys all centers

place your body in the pleasure of the other
and regain in your dance the breath of stars

without a center without a right or left
will your body be the sovereign orphan?
will you pirouette without losing your balance?

no bee's sting will distract me

meditate upon the bitter proof that I reveal to you
and if this argument doesn't stir the blood in your heart
then what can I do for you, poor fool?

renounce your uncontrollable joy

14.

to understand is to challenge four sources of power
the power of writing goes from the sign to its disappearance
the orthographic trace separates the hand from its root
the dance and the animated image overtake your body
the song and the music measure out your possibilities

hold to poetic knowledge without creating a fetish

what is "poetic knowledge"?
in writing you will protect thinking
in the orthographic trace you will reign over volatile motions
in music you will puncture living in time

a dry fig tree absorbs the singing of the stars
throw yourself laughing upon the straw of the wind

15.

the quality of the misery comes from the effort
that's why great misery is an orphan

in front of your eyes man dies like a swatted fly
and you cry like a bubbling fool

the class warrior never cries his solitude is furtive
he proudly kisses a cold excess

not one drop of blood merits your fury

you want the wealth of many
it's better to destroy the place where all wealth blooms
you dream of a strange transformation of the world
when will you dare to break from the singlemindedness
    of your desires?

meditate upon my vibratory discourse
because it dislodges the route of origins

16.

today is the awakening of your dead senses
but beware of this real pleasure
marijuana wine allow your negligence

to smoke when history seems to fail
consoles your easy cluelessness, poor fool!

to drink wine with your sleeves rolled up
helps a little your phallic leap
it's better to swallow the class warrior while dancing

I tell you this to drink in your spirit

stick to the aquatic mode of production

17.   the secret is to remain within the wound that is the world
that's why I'm infinitely orphaned
capable of destroying myself I break with the class enemy

hardships will never stop my trance-like violence

18.   the border between two countries is invisible
that's how I can merge with your language without losing
   myself

stick to the wild sound of the word "barbarous"

you will know the difference of difference
that your whirling jubilation will bring you
learn the language of the other
so that the language of your veins will be distilled

nothing can surpass the word "barbarous"
turned into a sword to fight sand

confront the rapidity of my language and learn

19.   those who stay in one place haven't dared live
those who travel without knowledge fall adrift

the rainbow in the sky repeats my wandering
and from cloud to cloud my words burn your steps

promise to your barbarity the flash of menace

20.

what makes one people the rival of another?
the rich crawl to money
the poor bleed from their bodies

to dominate is to put in play the final weapons
to distrust is to tremble from one's own horror
to break apart is to take pleasure from one's folly

I reveal this very simple thing to you
so that the class war redoubles its fury

sometimes the people rush forward
sometimes they slip in ignorance
sometimes they change in their disorder
sometimes they stick to constant virtues

so I teach you difference without return
and I add to your harp a resonant chord
I speak of your drunkenness sign after sign
I teach you everlasting pleasure

if all oppressed peoples took up arms
they would dance proudly on the class enemy

but pride is a word
used when talking

don't give in to the agile cruelty of my language
at every moment vacillate in the double mirror

the braid that you weave resounds on the vibratory sands

21.   how to defeat the usury of your historical being?
mobile ungraspable
you will confront the enemy while timing your breath

in appearing
take on the suppleness of the dancing reed

prisoner
cast off your personal fears
practice the asceticism of non-action

after the torture
demystify the torturers

O suicide
go back to fight the class enemy
or hit the open road
always nuance your aggression

because the subject of history is transitory
class war requires an orphan movement

because lasting critique dislodges your desires
action and knowledge collide and spark

open yourself to a radical divestment

22.

while talking about his wandering an ancient sage said
I don't know if the wind pushed me along or whether I
    pushed the wind

meditate upon this crystalline point of being

stranger to the center you displace things
stranger to origins you place value in the return
be it eternal

and so I walk with my head bowed
and so I wander a winged murderer

23.   whether male or female or androgynous
each term carries with it the two others
the void that unifies them incites your uncontrollable joy
to make love well is to tie together this volatile site
to make love well is to paint this void white
that's why I talk about making love to love

I heard it said
that each one of these terms is sufficient by itself
I heard this and I burst out laughing
why?
the more we focus on one term the more it shrinks
the more we valorize it the less we know ourselves
the closer we approach it the less we're our own masters
the suppleness of lovemaking resides in the combinatory

24.

the male falls seven times and gets up eight
the female half gives herself up and half enjoys herself

those who pivot with suppleness
will understand the orientation of the cosmos
those who make love with harmony
will discover the combinatory

a good male is a quadruped of incense
a good female is a vermilion ravine
a good androgyne unites the perfume to the jade

an ancient sage said
why do you worry about the Immortal Pill
when you can drink from the Fountain of Jade?

meditate upon this metaphor while pivoting
according to the rhythm of your desired positions

25.

imitating the style of the ancients
I disfigure their morality
altering their voice
I set free origins

the non-origin is at play in the origin
imitation requires distance
that's why I reject nothing
without having chewed some ginger

poor fool who refuses the secret of imitation
learn here learn these four principles
for reading and unreading a text:
identity of opposites
fragility of images
music of rhetoric and overdetermining rigor
therein lies the frame of the text

in imitating me you discover your difference

26.   this bread is hot this bread is round
that's why I eat joyfully

the one who laughs deafens the enemy
each laugh makes you sovereign

the warrior doesn't suck his mother's breast
nor his father's dick
he swallows them

eat this eat that
that's the secret of every act of eating

27.

the rain falls in the desert
once or twice a year
the bedouin gently caresses his camel
the supreme departure throbs on the horizon

the rupture of the voyage enlivens difference
but why insist upon this?
it's left up to people
to teach fasting to their kindred
it's up to them to leave origins behind

upon the doorstep of being your solitude quavers

to dance a jig to the rhythm of the universe
that's to discover the wisdom of wandering

to kiss the wisdom of wandering
that's to open up the body's fertile slope

while leaping learn the gyre of your desire

28.   set free your body quavers
wandering your body challenges the class enemy
that's why the illness
is the oblique doorway of your disorder
acupuncture upends class medicine

I heard it said
that dream science cures your illness
I heard that and I balled my fists

knowledge will never cure your irremediable distemper

every day and every night
while breathing swallow your neverending madness
that's the secret of every cure

29.   class war moves like a big wave
it can go right and left

the class warrior is born of this trembling
without origin
the class warrior takes sovereign action
without false rule
the class warrior takes hold of power
while decentering it

its force traces out a lasting critique

30.

the low tears down the high
the high raises the low
that's how authority crumbles

it will eliminate the external fury
so fury will devour it from the inside
it will neutralize the internal fight
so a delirious vacuity will ensue

because power is a continuous sharing
its overcoming requires an art of divestment
in the exercise of power be a vigilant bystander
I tell you this so you can conserve your energy

while pivoting listen to the reason of my song

31.   language of gold language of class
this is my first adage
knowing more is a class privilege
this is my second adage

being a class warrior is also a class virtue

reject all goals while transforming the world
this is the extreme secret of all utopias

my sentences are simple my word choice exact
the parable of the people inspires my singularity

32.

what makes a writer?
a good writer seduces first
poisons second
and in the course of writing
the writer poisons the writer

what makes a reader?
a good reader absorbs the poison
but doesn't die from pleasure
the reader creates a purer poison
absorbing the spirit of other readers

what makes a book?
a good book obeys the laws of transmigration
it has an orphan signature
it stands outside of its intimate uncontrollable joys

good writer good reader good book
this is still a class virtue

write while clawing at your crystalline voluptuousness

38.   the pure image quavers between two mirrors
that which remains plunges into the forgotten pleasure
how else to surprise the zither's sound?

nothing will ever fix in place my wandering

before I had to load the wind onto horses
now I have to rewrite history

while flying accentuate the shapeshifting of your body

39.   peaceful solitude nostalgic sadness strange sadness
I leave it up to vacuity to control their fervor

will someone cross beyond the veil of my hazel eyes?
will an orphan drifter like my dissipation?
will the aquatic vibrate in response to my drunkenness?

from the corner of my eye I see half of the universe

35.   identity difference
two words to point to the same knot

to untie these words is to trace out a spiral
to trace an elastic spiral in the body
is to enter into exile
to consign oneself wildly to the other
is to open oneself to difference without return

the singular and the plural touch the void
the mirror pivots on every cold surface
the being of a thousand layers trembles in front of my
    insouciance

here is where the sign and the sense explode again
and my veiled face agitates the water lily

a fiery ether illuminates difference without return
and I laugh uproariously when the wind hoists me up

36.
　　from the root to the branch
　　the bird flits
　　the wind is a whip
　　a word: is this "barbarous"?

　　know how to naturalize people joyfully in the universe!

　　exile beneath the rain
　　red flashes of lightning
　　luminous verse!
　　jade tears!

37.

constraints reign in the overflow
every hierarchy makes this so
every wisdom catches on fire
that's why surplus corrupts needs

production reproduction
capital work
the transformation of the world goes up in costly flames
excessive desire takes care of itself

the one who veers toward excess approaches the impossible
the one who looks at the impossible refigures the constraint

stick to an impossible mode of production

38.

capitalism socialism nationalism
every change of wording
requires a change in direction

we insult capital
but that's not enough to defeat it
we proclaim socialism
but we must always modify it
and sometimes nationalism liberates
sometimes it oppresses

how to fight then without losing ourselves?
know this:
now that action germinates in every body
and your body is changing directions
fling yourself toward the class enemy
and over and over display your fiery ardor
over and over draw the enemy in before pouncing

resolutely stick to the revolt of the woman

by acting repeat this repeat that
but each time beware of my rhetoric

when I cum into your mouth rinse out your mouth

39.   so here I exalt the word "death"
while the bird nearby cuts circles in the air
I come back to myself and look up at a white cloud

death riles me
like a night of lovemaking that makes me laugh

40.   and so I abandon the ordered course
and in this voyage I find my route
my little boat slips
the wave hits the dancing spume
time stops: the birds cry out against my fixed vision

no regret will interrupt my song
I leave you now in the azure vapor
I leave you
with my awkward shadow

sometimes we pivot against ourselves sometimes we avoid
    ourselves
sometimes freeing his wings the exile gets drunk
exiled from origins exiled from names exiled from history
and a plaything of difference the exile luxuriates in a strange
    suffering
this is the human lot

separating the reflections from their appearance
is given to them
separating the body from its violent symmetry
either in overwhelming the origin of their undecided reason
or in questioning the signs of human drifting
or in rupturing the mirror they exceed their being

so by three degrees the power rises over the spume
and a diaphanous wind accompanies my words
each time my words exile me to where the origin breaks off
each time I begin to speak I snap the consensus of thinking

isn't there then the emotion of the vibratory sign?
isn't there then the landscape traced out by my wandering?

leaning on the oar I lose track of my heart

there where the birds disappear I offer myself to flight
in the flecks of foam my form is changing
and the music is cold when my boat slips into the night

one note brings back the spume
I cross the night with my wet clothes
the voice that sings there emerges from a dream

my trembling hand is a pure image
a limpid color a glacial sign
and the pattern on the wave permits the moonlight

everywhere on this outing we call to nature
everywhere our orphaned being sings a barbarous song
isn't our heart a voluptuous flame?
our heart of a thousand layers?
our foot on a patch of grass?

to reach you I question the direction of the wind
only vacuity comes: trembling eyelashes!

sleep will soon bring me to the ocean's shore
a fresh morning will thrust me toward the beach
the country where I recognize the spurge's flower
and the gazelle's hooves

a hunter of sunken treasures squats at the desert's edge
turning around he stares at me
no doubt he wonders who I am
curious treasure treasure treasure
I sense his irony as he smiles and winks at me
to relieve my thirst he offers me camel's milk
while I drink he smokes looking at the sea
a gazelle runs over the sand my fatigue dissipates
the gazelle's femininity embraces my orphan suffering
white on white she touches my body's repose
white on white she kneels on the sand
parallel to the water
and in a drunken night
she will die
wanting to capture in the water
the moon's reflection

shaking out his pipe the treasure hunter says
unknown traveler you're not allowed to rest
the signs that lead you astray are pure intoxication
false mirror the beauty that beguiles you
renounce it
before it breaks you
forget your origins your childhood
the nomadic mirror is empty
your name is empty

the more a person travels the more the sign on the horizon
   crumbles
and the more laughable death becomes

upon every step a new shadow grabs you
you think you're living but you're just playacting in front of
   your mirror
and always seated I am like a grain of sand
travelers pass between the heavens and the earth
they forget
that the desert is an orphan truth

discover truth in its own desert
that's the first law of wandering

unknown traveler the sea spit you up at my feet
forget the sunken treasure and go on
I ask nothing of you praise God!

this text has a title and some allusions
it has a name
if someone has to step into the beyond, I'll volunteer

I'll steal the title of the orphaned sage

ABOUT THE AUTHOR

Abdelkébir Khatibi (1938–2009) was born in El Jadida, Morocco. After earning his PhD in sociology at the Sorbonne, he returned to live and work in Morocco. A writer of great breadth and challenging variety, Khatibi is known for works of literary and social criticism such as *Maghreb pluriel*, for experimental fiction such as *Amour bilingue*, for his anti-autobiography *La mémoire tatouée*, and for volumes of poetry including *Le lutteur de classe à la manière taoïste* and *Aimance*.

Matt Reeck is co-translator, with Aftab Ahmad, of Mushtaq Ahmed Yousufi's *Mirages of the Mind* (New Directions), selected as one of the twenty-five best translations of 2016 by Three Percent, and of Saadat Hasan Manto's *Bombay Stories* (Vintage), chosen by the *New York Times* as a 2014 editor's choice. He has won grants from the Fulbright Foundation, the National Endowment for the Arts, and the PEN/Heim Fund.